POEMS I STOLE FROM MY IMAGINARY FRIENDS

BY JORGE MENDEZ

Wider Perspectives Publishing ¤ 2023 ¤ Hampton Roads, Va.

The poems and writings in this book are the creations and property of Jorge Mendez; the author is responsible for them as such. Wider Perspectives Publishing reserves 1st run rights to this material in this form, all rights revert to author upon delivery. Author reserves all rights thereafter: Do not reproduce without permission except Fair use practices for approved promotion or educational purposes. Author may redistribute, whole or in part, at will, for example submission to anthologies or contests.

© January 2023, Jorge Mendez, Virginia Beach, VA.
Wider Perspectives Publishing, Hampton Roads
ISBN 978-1-952773-66-2

For Jeff and Delaney

contents

1   Imaginary Friends
2   Identity

THE BOSS

8   Adversaries
10   Bully
12   Treadmill Recliner
14   Hello Darkness
16   Break
19   Pins and Needles
20   Closet
22   Heroes
24   Grief
27   Over-Achiever
28   Inkblot
35   These Old Poems
37   Growing Pains
39   Oak
40   Under Construction
42   The Mutiny of My Belongings

THE HOPELESS ROMANTIC

48   Quitters
49   Adventure Seeker
52   More Day
55   Unattended Funeral
56   Driftwood
58   This Girl
60   Threat Level 143
63   Prepare for Launch
65   Revelation
67   Show and Tell
68   Undeserved
70   Amusing My Muse
75   Carnival
79   Happy (Triple Haiku)
80   Technicolor Anti-Muse
84   A Brief List of Things I Know
88   Semi-Broken Things

THE QUIET ONE

92   Dear Silence
94   Shadow
95   Decals
96   On the Bone
98   Predator and Prey
99   Extinction Level Neo-Genesis
101 Lines
103 The Growl
105 Autumn Stew
106 Luna
109 Soul of August
111 Rockface
112 Alphabet Soup
114 Crescendo
116 Neon Bus Stop
119 The City Breathes in Technicolor
120 Gray
121 Astro Aquarian

THE JESTER

124	Nemesis	138	Tommy Boy
125	A Letter from Igloo	140	Retail Employee's Holiday Prayer
127	Cellular Degeneration		
130	A Call from Beyond	141	Teddy's New Roommate
132	About Last Night	143	Tug, Yank, Tear
133	Covert Ops	145	Poem's Ad
136	Fungus	146	Poem Responds to Ad

THE GIRL

150	Failure	164	Coming Soon
151	Instructions for Putting Together a Puzzle	166	On Fire
		167	Cockroach
152	Monster House	168	The Price
153	True Colors	169	Misunderstood Mountain
154	Purple	171	66 Questions for God
156	We All Keep Secrets	178	Human Deities
157	Rage Review	180	Broadcasting
159	BLM	181	Somedays
160	Exit Newtown North		

THE CHILD

184	Curfew Was a Streetlight	198	To the Dreams I Can't Remember
187	Caterpillars		
188	Endangered Species	199	Galactose
189	Life Saver	202	The Previews
191	Orphans	205	The Seed
194	Just	207	Sparrow
195	Play Date	209	The Last Laugh
196	Recess	212	10 Reasons

113	About the Author

Imaginary Friends

My friends and I
have sat here together.

Silently.

Hours at a time.

Trying to figure out
which one of us
is the imaginary one. . .

Jorge Mendez

Identity

...and I use the word "friends" loosely.
I mean, we know each other,
but only in passing,
the way
salt knows ocean air.

Most times,
I can barely even make out their faces.
Whether in the mirror
or the window
or the puddle.

One looks like the Boss though.
Clearly, he's the one in charge
or at least thinks he is.
Stern, intense.
Feigns strength
for the sake of the others.
He's holding a clipboard.
I'm not sure what he's writing down,
but I hear the pen grinding against the paper.
It sounds furious.
Like voices in broken homes.
Like brakes at the last minute.
He screams at the top of his lungs,
not because he's angry,

but because he's terrified.
I pretend to not know why.

Then there's the Hopeless Romantic,
who loves as if he knows
his life depends on it.
Loves,
even when against his
own best interest.
The heart on his sleeve,
battle worn
decorated with puncture wounds
defiantly still beats.
Loudly.
Profoundly.
Undeterred and fully prepared
to pour itself out again. . .
and again…
and again...

There's one who keeps his face hidden.
Only shows me the top of his head.
Eyes fixed to the ground.
Admires his feet,
wonders where they'll take him.
He looked up once, but couldn't handle the glare.
Keeps his eyes covered these days,
but that doesn't seem
to keep him from seeing.

Jorge Mendez

He's just learned to be selective
of what he allows catch his gaze.
He's quiet, not silent
and prefers to absorb
rather than expel.
It's been said,
"He thinks too much."
He's never understood what that means.

Another,
smiles like he knows the punchline
to a joke I haven't told.
Laughs much too late.
Doesn't seem to take
anything seriously.
He's both the jester and
the butt of the joke.
He just snickered because
he heard me say, "butt".
Immature.
Sophomoric.
Sometimes he's too much.
Sometimes he's not enough.

The girl
is loving, but fierce.
She is the advocate.
The voice of reason,
the wailing cry for justice.
Blanket Guardian.

The strongest one among us
because she feels the deepest.
They say all men have a feminine side.
Mine just so happens
to wear the pants.
I believe she will be
the one who saves us.

The youngest one,
the child, is my favorite.
Sings out of key.
Doesn't care.
Just Sings louder.
Wears a towel around his neck like a cape.
It's where he gets his powers.
Lives in a blanket fort.
The walls are impervious.
He tucks me behind the sheets,
holds my face in his tiny hands and tells me
that as long as I stop growing up, I'll be safe here.

He makes drawings of the rest of us.
All with the same face.
Draws me holding a tissue,
and wearing a towel around my neck.

Jorge Mendez

THE BOSS

*. . . He screams at the top of his lungs.
not because he's angry,
but because he's terrified . . .*

Adversaries

We've grappled
back and forth
for decades
haven't we?
Lifelong adversaries
born of the same
cruel cloth.
You, devourer of glow, heavy handed.
Me,
infected by your shadow,
stubborn and
unrelenting.
This eternal
tit for tat
between us.
You swing,
connect.
I absorb the blow,
swing back.
You seem unaffected.

This goes on infinitely
until either you best me
or I find the strength
to fight you off.

Usually, the former.
        Mostly the former.

I've become used to this.
Accustomed even.
Comfortable,
if I could be
so bold.

Jorge Mendez

Bully

My depression
greets me
like a school yard bully.
Calls me names.
Bruises my ego.
It doesn't want
my lunch money.
It wants
my appetite,
and it gets it.

    Sometimes,
        for days at a time.

I feel no haunting ache
in my gut.
No growl in my belly.
I've known hunger pains before,
that's not what this is.

This
is not starvation.
At least,
not in a biological sense,
but I'm famished
nonetheless.

Despite the buffet
my plate is a bounty
of things
I have no taste for.

Jorge Mendez

Treadmill Recliner

Brain on a treadmill.
Body in a recliner.
Stuck somewhere
between tired
and wired.

Electric.
Power surging.
While my eyelids
bench press
my lashes.

The weight
of yesterday
turns today into plaster
while tomorrow

         waits.

The mind
is dormancy's nightmare.
I'm restless,
searching for the
cool side of the pillow
on the dark side
of morning.

Sleep
died somewhere
in an I.V. drip.
Insomnia taps the vein.

Jorge Mendez

Hello Darkness

Oh,
there you are.
I've been expecting you.
I felt the melancholy brewing
in our bones,
smelled
the familiar aroma of sorrow simmering.
I knew you'd come knocking soon.
It's been a while,
good for you.

So,
what is it this time?
Money troubles?
Feeling unaccomplished?
Didn't get the girl?
Oh, that struck a nerve.
So, it's a girl then?
Yes, of course it is,
let me guess:
It's the raven-haired one isn't it.
I recognize her calling card
in your tear tracks.
I can always count on her
to send you running back
into the shadow of my embrace.

There, there.
What did she do this time?
Not return a text?
Insult you?
Reject you?
…again?

I'm sorry.
That was unfair,
but come on,
it's like you do it on purpose.
As much as you claim to hate me
you sure do go out of your way
to fall back into me.

Admit it,
you like it in the dark,
joke about how it matches your soul
though you've always looked
better in blues.
Your melancholy majesty,
wearing your insecurities like royal garb,
depression like a bejeweled crown.
Sew heartache into the
emperor's new clothes so
you can show it off on stage.

Jorge Mendez

Nothing pushes your pen
quite like a fresh rejection.
Nothing moves the audience
quite like anguish on display
and no one,
and I mean no one,
weaves a tale of woe
quite like you do,
tortured poet.

That's why
you're really back,
you need a new poem.
You're a writer.
That means you can bleed out
and never die.
So, bleed.
Wallow in your words
to feel worthwhile.
Bleed!
Search for validation
in the snaps of fingers.
Bleed!
Carry the weight of your existence
in every verse you utter!

Sell It boy!
Force them to feel you!
Command them to cheer with every tear

that plummets from your cheek,
invoke envy of your torment,
hurt so good
you make them jealous,
spit that sorrow
'til it hits the mic like a symphony,
leave it all on stage to burn
under the heat of the lights
until they explode into
a crescendo of applause boy,
Bleed!

All
      the
            way
                   out.

After all,
the pain
is worth the poem,
right?

Jorge Mendez

Break

Sometimes,
when you feel yourself breaking,
you just need a break.

Other times,
you need to break something.

Some things
are worth repairing,
others
are better left broken.

Rarely,
do we break-even.
Rarely,
is it clean.
There is typically rubble
at the sight of the fracture.

I mean,
it makes sense, doesn't it?
Where else would I break
if not at my fault line?

The real question is,
where does the fault lie?

Pins and Needles

There's a callous complexity
to feeling everything
and nothing all at once.
The flood of emotion
and simultaneous vacancy
when you reach into
a bag of fucks
and find it empty.
        None left to give.
            Not even the one
                you were saving for yourself.

Odd as it may seem
it hurts worse
once you've gone numb.
You fall asleep
the way a foot does,
on pins and needles.

You need rest,
but sleep won't help
when it's your soul
that's tired.

Jorge Mendez

Closet

Cleaning out a closet
is warrior work.
The epic battle between
"I no longer need this…" and
"…but someday I might."
is a merciless one.
Filling a Hefty Cinch Sack
with old baggage
is anything but a cinch.

When you find an old rejection
in the pocket of a hoodie
you wore the last time you
felt lonely,
or when your favorite shirt
is now a size of happiness
you don't fit into,
it can be easy to feel like a
Hand-Me-Down.

You never did shake
that pebble from your shoe,
but you don't plan to walk in them
anymore, anyway…
do you?

Thrift shops are just
halfway homes
for donated emotions.
Shelves full of secondhand acceptance.
Bargain bins full of yesterdays.

Letting go is never easy,
but neither is holding on.
The bag is heavy,
the work is tedious,
but just think of
all the space
you'll make.

Heroes

One
by
one
my heroes
are laying down their capes,
removing their
utility belts,
and flying away.

Their departure,
villainous.
Kryptonite.
A weakness inducing
sucker punch
to the heart.
Bane's knee
in the spine of The Bat.

I'm dusted
by the snap of a finger.

However,
their powers remain.
Here.
Within the red walls
of our fortress,

though for the moment
I need solitude.

At least,
until I grow to fit their capes.
Until I don't disappear
into their boots.

Jorge Mendez

Grief

...so, I'm learning
that grief is nonlinear.
There is no start
or finish.
No beginning
or end.
That it's more of
an ebb and flow.
A rise and
a fall.
That it has a
nonchalant,
come and go
sort of existence.

I'm learning
that grief
doesn't visit.
It resides.
Once it's crossed
your threshold
it never leaves the house.
It settles in.
It makes itself comfortable.
It lives with you now.

I'm learning
grief is not
a process.
It's not something
you go through,
but more something you sit in.
It is permanent.
It is footprints in cement.
Initials in a tree trunk.
It is Tattoo ink.

I'm learning
that grief is indecisive.
It gets better
then it gets worse.
It gets better
then it gets worse.
It gets worse.
It gets worse.
It gets better...

I'm told
that eventually
it graduates to 'ok'
and settles into 'manageable',
but as of right now
'manageable'
is an unattainable,

Jorge Mendez

mythic, relic lost
somewhere unreachable.
As of right now
'manageable'
feels clumsy
on my tongue.

Captain,
you taught me many things,
but this is a lesson
I'd rather not have learned.
In this I wish
for ignorance,
but I'm still learning...

Over-Achiever

It feels like grief just took the weekend off.

It's back on the clock today.

Putting in extra hours.

Working
through its lunch
break.

Like it wants a fucking promotion.

Jorge Mendez

Inkblot

She invites me to lay down on the couch,
I choose not to.

She holds up a white flash card with a black inkblot,
asks me what I see.
I say, "gray."

"No" she says, "I mean what does this look like to you?"
I say, "an amoeba."

This frustrates her.
I've been coming to her long enough where I can tell.
She huffs a bit through her nose,
turns her head as though
she's just about to shake it in dismay,
but catches herself.
I can see the word smart-ass
hanging from the tip of her tongue
like a suicide jumper that had a change of heart.
Something inside her mouth grabs it and sucks it back in
like a spaghetti noodle.
She makes a face like it tastes bad.
All this happens within a fraction of a second,
but I've picked up on it.

I frustrate her quite a bit.
I feel bad about that honestly,

but I don't do it intentionally.
I mean,
insurance only covers so much
and I'm not coming out of pocket
just to play mind games with a shrink.
… but I come here with questions,
hoping to find answers and instead
she asks me more questions.
Now that's just counterproductive.

"...and why do you think that is Jorge?"

How should I know why that is?
That's what I'm paying you 129 dollars an hour to figure out!
But I don't say that out loud.

I don't say much out loud at all and that's why she gets frustrated.
Maybe I should just let her read my notebooks and get back to me?

Once she's masked her flicker of frustration she starts again.
She's so patient with her patients.
She holds up another card and asks once more,
"Jorge. Really, what do you see?"

As I begin to form yet another smart-ass answer
the corners of my mouth start creeping upwards
and like I said, I've been coming to see her for quite some time
so, while she may not know what I'm going to say
she knows that she won't like it
and she's not having it.

Jorge Mendez

Before I can say anything at all
she forces the card down onto her desk and lets me have it.

"Enough Jorge! Enough!
I have exhausted myself trying to help you,
but neither I,
nor anyone else,
not even The Almighty God can help you
unless you want to help yourself.
You've been coming into my office
twice a week,
for an hour,
for the last seven months
and we've made no progress whatsoever.
I've administered every test and conducted every evaluation ever developed
in the field of mental health.
I've employed every tool given to me in my 6 years of college education.
I've called colleagues to ask for suggestions on ways to approach you.
I'm administering a fucking Rorschach Test,
for Christ's sake Jorge,
do you have any idea how outdated that is?"

She pauses.

Face flush.
Jaw muscle flexed.
Lips pursed so tight they've turned white.

She breathes in through her nose
as though she's attempting
to syphon all the air out of the room
in hopes I might suffocate.
Fixes her glasses
which had shifted slightly on her face during her tempest,
smiles with false politeness,
then leans back in her chair
like nothing happened.

"Now listen to me, ok?
I'm going to ask you one more time
so, humor me.
What...do...you...see?"

In the back of my mind I'm thinking,
"Woooow! and you think I might be bi-polar?"
But I don't say that out loud.

Instead, I say this:

"Well,
when I do see through the tears, I see pain.
I see heartache.
I see love only briefly then lose sight of it quick.
I see loneliness so deep it has an echo.
I see the moon of my soul glowing pale being bombarded by asteroids.
I see my veins being injected with trust from a dirty syringe.
I see myself being spoon-fed hope laced with cyanide,

Jorge Mendez

and I gobble it up like an idiot.
I see people smiling at me in the light but,
their shadows have horns and cloven hooves
and I am afraid of them.
I see "kick me" signs in a pat on the back,
Joy buzzers in handshakes,
and people that would help me up the mountain
just to push me off the cliff.
I see false motives in good deeds.
Resentment in rainbows.
Contempt in a bowl of ice cream.
I am a cynical,
sarcastic,
bitter bastard
it's no wonder I'm alone
and I don't understand
how you don't see that...

...You just keep giving me drugs,
but maybe I don't need pills
maybe all I need's a hug?

If I'm not here or at work,
I'm at home in my room,
sitting by myself on my bed
thinking incessantly.
My headboard has a mirror on it
and directly across from it
so does my dresser
so, when I look at my reflection

it just bounces back and forth infinitely
between the two panes of polished glass
making me smaller
and smaller
and smaller
and smaller
and smaller
as the tunnel drags my image away
to wherever it is
that images get dragged to.

I know I've been coming here
twice a week,
for an hour,
for seven months,
and I know I keep saying I want you to help me,
but I don't let you.

I know.

…but I only left my house
for 40 hours a week
before I started seeing you
and for the last seven months you've made it 42.
So yes, I've dragged it out on purpose
and I've refused to throw you bones
because these sessions
twice a week are the only times
I'm not alone.

Jorge Mendez

So, there it is.
That's what I see.
Now that you've gotten
what you want from me,
my hour's up and
I'm still down,
but thank you for your company.

These Old Poems

These old poems,
band aids
I forgot to remove
grafted to my
adolescent skin.
Peel back
layers upon layers
of unaddressed
memories.
Blocks that built a
broken wordsmith.
The literary DNA
of my poetic make up.
The spines of every
spiral bound notebook
double helix.

I had no idea
what I was getting
myself into.
The dust I'd kick up.
The heartache I'd unearth.
The wounds I'd reopen
or the new scars
I'd discover
incubating

Jorge Mendez

between the
tattered covers
of these relic journals.

I should
have done this sooner,
and somehow simultaneously,
not have done this at all.

Growing Pains

I bet it hurts like Hell
when a caterpillar's
wings break through
its back.

Maybe I just think too much?

Maybe it's the moon
playing with my mood,
tugging on my malaise
like high tide?

Nah,
I definitely think too much.

Most times,
just trying to think up ways
to stop thinking.

Trapped in my own head,
thoughts beating against
the inside of my skull.
Lunatic ideas
throwing themselves
against the bone.
Why must the cranium
be so damn resilient?

Jorge Mendez

I need to get the fuck out of here!

Change often hurts.
They call them growing pains
for a reason.
They say,
it builds character.

That would explain
why my back aches.

I'm just not sure if
I'm carrying too
heavy a load,
or if I'm finally
sprouting wings.

Oak

My limbs
breathe deep,
absorb the color
from my leaves.

Drain them until they
brittle and brown
and blanket at my feet.

I take root
in all that is rich.

My toes dirty, but
firmly planted.

A bite far
less threatening than
my bark.

Something
lives within me.

I find comfort
being shelter.

Jorge Mendez

Under Construction

I suppose,
I needed to defend myself.
These walls of self-preservation
weren't going to
build themselves,
but
I'm no architect.
No carpenter
with God like workmanship.
No crafty bricklayer.
I don't know
who I think I'm fooling here.

I've never felt
at home within this
fleshy dwelling.

These walls
have been
crumbling
for some time now.
Floorboards dusty and
dead with dry rot.
The roof has
slit its wrist
and bled the rain.

The foundation
is exhausted
of being strong.
This is no shelter.

It's time
to set it on fire,
burn it all down,
and rebuild.

Jorge Mendez

The Mutiny of My Belongings

I wonder what my pillows think of my dreams.
Does the ground get angry when I drag my feet?
I wonder if my ink thinks I'm insane.
What do the walls of my apartment say
when I'm not home
and are my clothes ashamed to be seen with me in public?
I mean,
they probably know me better than anyone.

Drawers and closets hide my secrets
and baskets of dirty laundry,
but I'm afraid they're about to blow the whistle.
At night I hear them whispering to the lamps.
Clandestine partnerships with light bulbs
conspiring to air out my inefficiencies
and cast light into the
shadows I've been hiding in.

I can hear my skeletons getting restless
from behind the closet door.
The sound of bones rattling
is like an angry machine gun
with a stutter
struggling to find the right words.

I think my shoes are sick of carrying me.
Laces have dry rotted,
soles worn paper thin from baring
the weight of my own soul,
cumbersome and heavy
like a nomad's backpack.
For a while they kept me running,
now my feet are spewing
chunks of sock, sneaker, and shoelace
hurling them in violent,
clumsy bursts
like a rim
would the rubber
of a blown-out tire.
They're going to force me to walk on my own,
barefoot over the coals
and my tissues have turned against me.

My eyelids feel like the levies
in New Orleans
attempting to hold the line
against this hurricane of tears,
bulging off my face
swollen and red like I'm suffering from
an allergic reaction to my own masculinity.

My mirror can't stand the sight of me
so, he fogs over and
refuses to cast my reflection

as the voice inside it sneers
"You're not ready".
I Wipe away the steam with my forearm
to reveal the polymorphic,
deformed, funhouse mirror version of myself
where my frown somehow becomes a smile
and I'm able to step thru my front door
to face you all.

Out here,
tears become laughter,
scars transform into tattoos,
and sob stories turn into humorous anecdotes.
You chuckle with the me I show you
until I cross the thresh hold
back into my home.

As I slide the key into the lock
the rumbles of gossip
fall to a whisper
and I swear I hear the closet mumble,
"Shh, he's coming".
The walls suppress their giggles
like shy schoolgirls,
light bulbs dim their filaments,
and the mirror
attempts to remind me who I am...

...but in this moment,
on a night like tonight,

still high off the love you've all given me,
I start to feel like maybe me is not so bad.

I peel away my embarrassed garments,
yank off my tired shoes,
smash the mirror,
drag my skeleton out of the closet
onto the front lawn by the throat,
and stand there naked
with the door wide open.
Scared.
Crying.
Exposed,
but ready to invite you in.

THE HOPELESS ROMANTIC

*...loves as if he knows
his life depends on it.
Loves,
even when against his
own best interest...*

Jorge Mendez

Quitters

You quit me
the same week
I quit cigarettes.

There's a poem
in there somewhere.

It's either
in the ash
or in the smoke.

Adventure Seeker

I loved you like a fairy tale.
I, your Prince Valiant,
released you from your tower of discontent.
I washed away your witches,
defeated your dragons
I gobbled up your goblins.
You,
said I was your hero.

I took you by your hand
and lead you safely through
the wilderness of your apprehensions,
beyond the forest of self-doubt,
across the violent rivers of your past
to an open field of
jasmine possibilities,
lilac daydreams,
and hibiscus hopes.

I dressed your wounds
I nourished your emaciated self-esteem,
kept you fed on a balanced diet of
compliments, positive affirmations, and affection
until you were strong enough to fend for yourself,
but little did I know, that once you got your bearings
you'd run off seeking adventure.

Jorge Mendez

…but last, I remember,
your last adventure
got you locked away in a tower.

Still, you said you needed time
so, I surrendered my calendar
and arm wrestled the hands of every clock I could find.
You asked for space
so, I sent you on an all-expense paid tour of the galaxy,
but even on a road trip through the cosmos
you complained about the potholes.

You never were satisfied,
and I knew this.

Even so, I carried a slow burning lantern
along the rings of Saturn
dripping beads of wax hoping to create
a constellation you'd be happy with.

I treated you like you were my very most current breath
so much more precious than the last,
with the knowledge that each breath
could be my last.
I cherished you.

I kept you exalted
catching crooks in my neck
every time I'd try to look at you

perched so perfectly on the pedestal I placed you on.
So blinded by the glare,
I didn't even notice when you fell,
but still caught you just in time
to no longer recognize
what I was saving.

I should have let you hit the ground.
I should have let you hurt yourself.
In the end,
we would have both been better off.

Jorge Mendez

More Day

The truth is
I still think of you.
Everyday.
Somedays more than others
but every day, nonetheless.
…and today?
Today is a "more" day.

I stumbled on
a memory of you while
rummaging through a drawer.
Now I can't remember
what I was searching for
in the first place.

This.
Happens.
Much too often.

Just the other day,
while looking for the number to the Italian spot
across the street,
I scrolled
past your name
in my address book
and lost my appetite.
I still haven't found it.

It's been days.

I haven't written
a worthwhile word
almost 3 months.
It's like you took my
creativity with you when you left.
You went from muse to poltergeist,
your phantoms haunting my pen.
Now every word that falls to paper
has your ghost in it,
but there's never been a ritual
for exercising this type of demon.
No amount of holy water
that could wash away
the sin that was
my faith in you.
No matter how hard I scrub,
I still can't get you
from underneath my finger nails.

I've tried everything.

Sometimes
you resurface as
a lump in my throat
and I remember
in those moments how
you made me promise
to never write our breakup poem.

Jorge Mendez

…but this is not a breakup poem.
This is not a broken heart poem.
This is not a bitter poem.
This is not a poem at all.
This is a distress call.
I'm drowning
a million miles off the coast
of I miss you with nothing
but your goodbye for a life vest
and that shit's full of holes.

Fingers and feet pruned,
by now,
you'd expect I'd finally
learn to swim
or just fucking drown already
from all the saltwater
in my lungs.

I can't breathe
so, I just float here.

I just want to forget you,
but the pieces of me that remain
keep calling out to the parts of you
that made me whole

and I still can't remember
what I was looking for.

Unattended Funeral

I wandered
the winding corridors
of our catacombs.

Exhumed the corpse.

Slept in the carcass
of yesterday.

I carried the stench
of our cadaver
like purgatory.

Wore it like
a tailored suit
fresh and
fit for burial.

In the distance
church bells
called for us
to attend mourning mass,

but neither of us
showed up for
the funeral.

Jorge Mendez

Driftwood

I cried for you today,
just as hard as
I did the day you left

and what I found
was that sometimes
the tears just flow smoother
than the ink does,
but then my poems
just soak into my pillowcase.

…and I must have written
a world worth of words
hoping the flow of ink
would eventually create the river
that would carry you back to me
like a message in a bottle
written on a day
when I was more
than just a piece of
driftwood to you.
On a day when the currents
flowed like colors
from your brush
so, you could paint
the moonbeams
back into my smile,

the mountain
back in my spine,
the pulse
back into my wrist.

When you left
my voice went with you
and I couldn't cry out to you
for months.
I miss you.
Don't hold it against me
and I won't blame you for it.
Some things are just
beautifully painful
you see?

I cried for you today,
just as hard as
I did the day you left
and I swear to you
I've never felt more alive.

Jorge Mendez

This Girl

So, there's this girl…
At least, I think she's a girl.
I'm actually not quite sure she's even human
because come to think of it,
I don't remember ever seeing her feet touch the ground.
There is a cushion of air
that exists somewhere between the earth
and the soles of her feet.
She doesn't walk,
she hovers.
I'm sure of it.

This girl
has sonnets in here smile and
limericks in her laughter,
moves quick like haiku,
with soliloquies in her footsteps.
She lives her life
in free verse.
She is a masterpiece,
no canvas worthy of
her image.
I have her paintings
hanging on the insides
of my eyelids.

This girl
has the curves
of a hand-crafted mandolin and
I'd strum her until she
produced the perfect song
or cried the sweetest melody.
MY GOD
This girl.
This girl
is a walking wet dream
I have while wide awake.

This girl
is in my thoughts like breathing is.
Natural.
Subconscious.
Continuous.
…and this girl
has no idea
I exist.

Jorge Mendez

Threat Level 143

There has been
a breach
to my
Se
Se
security systems interface.

I was not
programmed
to properly process
this emo
Mo
Mo
Mo
motion.

This flutter
in my circuitry
is Fa
Fa
Fa
foreign to me.

I am made of
cold steel alloy.
This warm feeling
in my motherboard

simply does not
Not
Not
Not
compute.

I deal solely
in that which
is logical and this
emotion does not
Oh
Oh
obey
the protocol.

When I focus
my optic sensors
upon her
I feel a
Wa
Wa
warmth begin to
radiate within me
even though I was never
Fi
Fi
fitted for heat coils.

Nothing in my
Da

Jorge Mendez

Da
databank
has prepared me
to engage in
the irrational.

There has been
a breach
to my
Se
Se
security systems interface.

Threat level 143.

Initiate self-destruct sequence
3
    2
        1....

Prepare for Launch

Wanna play a game of
Hop-scotch on
the surface of the moon?
A leap of faith
is boundless there.

How about a few rounds
of Hide and Seek
in the blush of
Jupiter's cheek?
Polaris
can be home base,
"Olly Olly
Oxen Free".

We could
Double Dutch
through a quasar.

Pin the Tail
on the comet.

Strap a saddle
to a rocket
and ride an
asteroid bronco
across the solar system
like a couple of

Jorge Mendez

space cowboys.
Corral the cosmos.

We could
Ring-Around-the-Rosy
on a loop of Orion's Belt
until
ashes
ashes
we
both
fall
into
one another's gravitational pull.

Or,
we can stop
acting like space cadets
and get down to the science.

Create friction.
Accelerate atoms.
Implode black holes.
Supernova.
Form stardust.
Inhale cosmic.
Breathe galactic.
Breed life
and become
interstellar.

Revelation

Pardon me miss but,
may I belong to you?
Would you mind too terribly,
being my deity?
I've already gone through
all the trouble of
building you this alter
and if you'd be so kind as
to allow me to worship you,
I'd surrender myself
to sacrifice right here
at your pulpit.

My love,
this cup,
it runneth over.
Let us sip from it together
and baptize our lips
as we create
a new religion.
We will be the only members
of this church
as our bodies both
commit the sin
and absolve ourselves of it
simultaneously.

Jorge Mendez

Let Me be
your disciple.
My fingertips following
your curves like commandments.
Celebrate your scriptures
like your second coming.
Arrive
at the steps of your temple.
Humble.
My head in your lap
whispering prayers
into your waist from
within the walls
of your confessional
until I am
born again!

Save me!

Say you'll be my Goddess
and give me
a revelation.

Show and Tell (A Villanelle)

Your flesh knows my secrets all too well.
Blanket blindfold, braille between the sheets.
I'm sure you have some tragedies to tell.

I have a yarn or two that I can sell,
a tapestry of words and disbelief.
Your flesh knows my secrets all too well.

Your story hiding, shy beneath your shell.
Rumors flutter when the tongue is weak.
I'm sure you have some tragedies to tell.

Purgatory promises, a roundtrip talk through Hell,
from within me somewhere limbo speaks.
Your flesh knows my secrets all too well.

The rise of tide when darkness fell
and shadows lapped around your feet.
I'm sure you have some tragedies to tell.

My voice is at a rebel's yell,
your dial is set to meek,
Your flesh knows my secrets all too well.
I'm sure you have some tragedies to tell.

Jorge Mendez

Undeserved

It almost
seems as though
these poems
don't deserve you.

Never
in the vastness
of all that is infinite,
could one articulate
the arrangement of words
to accurately describe
the heights of how
You love.

No metaphor,
however delicately crafted,
would ever be
so clever
that it could rival
You.

You
are a sonnet in sentiment.
A haiku
packed writhe and tight,
deliberately sculpted.

You
are unreachable
yet approachable.
Untouchable
in your rarity.

Syllables
will spin for you.
Meter
will curtsy
and verses
will sing your praise,
but the lyrics
will always be
unworthy.

These poems
don't deserve you,
but stanza
by stanza
they try
nonetheless.

Jorge Mendez

Amusing My Muse

When I met you
it wasn't like I met you,
it was more like I remembered.
The delicate harmonies of your voice
and subtle cadence of your speech
transported me
to a long-lost distant memory,
perhaps even from a previous life,
of someone
that I must have loved already.

You reminded me of things
I didn't know I had forgotten.
Things that up until this point
I would have sworn were impossible,
but you have me
questioning everything.
… and I'm learning…
that under the right conditions
I can fly.
I can move through walls.
I can push my pen across
the surface of the page
with my mind to write things
I hope,
amuse my muse.

Things like:
You're every colors favorite hue.
You're an autumn mountain's view.
A crossword puzzle clue.
A wind chime's favorite tune.
You're a brand-new pair of shoes,
I mean,
I want to walk with you.

I want to write poems
on every mirror in your house
so, when you look into them
you'll see what I see.
I want to be the fountain to your smile.
I want to tap your sense of humor
so, I can drink your laughter from a cup
and get drunk on your silly.
Let me get inebriated on
your most intimate ideas.
Let me be the goblet
you pour yourself into.
It is not enough to exist as
a part of your life,
I need to participate
in your existence.

Because every morning,
I wake up with your
song on my lips
and your name on my pillowcase.

Jorge Mendez

You're in the fibers
of every muscle I stretch,
arms extended reaching out for you.
You are my first sip of coffee,
you make me alert.
My mind's breakfast,
nourishment for good mornings,
and I can't think
of any better way
to start my day.

Last night I had a dream
that I was chasing you
through the empty hallways of an old hotel.
Listening for your giggle around corners
as I navigated the corridors,
following the trail of love letters
that fell out of your pockets.
When I caught you,
you handed me a notebook of blank pages
then ran off again,
leaving me counting backwards from ten,
singing catch me if you can.

So, I set my snares
and baited my hooks
within its pages
poetry poised
waiting to pounce on you,
but words just don't seem

worthy of you these days.
So instead, I leave treasures
mounted to walls
that only you would think to hunt for.
Only you could know their value.
Verbal trinkets
for you to add to your collection.
Vintage memories
we haven't yet created
and somehow,
the shoebox
we keep them in
is already over-flowing.
It's taking both of us to force the lid down
and even that's barely working.
Every phone call
is another love note
on a napkin.
Every message
a ticket stub
to a movie we haven't seen.
Every spoken word between us
falls perfectly into place
building something
we have no definition for.
Something so beautiful,
neither of us understand it but,
like a flower that blooms in the shade, though
the odds are against us,
we flourish.

Jorge Mendez

Our roots grow longer,
stronger,
uprooting the cobblestones
of the paths we once walked together.

Yes!
The paths we ONCE walked together.
This isn't the first time that
I've loved you.
It just can't be.
I told you,
I remember.

Carnival

Our
love
smiles
out
loud.

It sounds
like carnival music.

Silly,
boisterous,
and in just the right octave
to border on obnoxious.

Our love,
is the push of wind
against cheeks on
a roller coaster drop,
the force
that drives stomachs
up into throats.
A fearless free fall.

Our love
is honeysuckle snuggle.
Fingers snug between knuckles.
Knees buckle

Jorge Mendez

'til you belt one out...
keep your pants on,
I'm getting to the good part.

I say,
Gods have written volumes
on our love,
millennia into the future.
Our love
is not confined
to any comprehensible
plane of existence.

Our love is rare
like shooting stars,
blue diamonds,
or four-leaf clovers.
A lucky charm.
The prize
at the bottom of
my cereal box.
Something
to look forward to
like a horizon
or a punchline.

Our love is funny.

It laughs like
sidewalk chalk,

giggles the way
doodles do.
A sound I've grown addicted to.

Our love is
new-age narcotic.

It lays me to rest
humble head upon your chest,
I breathe easy.
It is my inhaler when
calamity claims my lungs
I say,
I breathe
easy.

Our love,
stirs me awake
draws me from slumber
whispers, "good morning".
My favorite
alarm clock.

Our love
speaks body language.
Breathes without lungs.

It's midnight Ben & Jerry's runs,
movie nights,
and cheap take out.

Jorge Mendez

It is
The Game of Life,
The Book of Life,
Fail Videos,
and Blacklist.
It is
Sloppy Joe's,
chips and dip,
and pickles
straight from the jar.
It's blanket forts,
Belle Isle,
and bad cooking shows.

Our love is silly and
a little bit ridiculous.

It smiles out loud,
it sounds like a carnival,
like festivities
and it is celebrating!

Happy (Triple Haiku)

I am so happy
that I have gained a few pounds.
That's not sarcasm.

I mean, not happy
that I have gained a few pounds.
Sorry, that's unclear.

What I mean to say
is I have gained a few pounds
because I'm happy.

Jorge Mendez

Technicolor Anti-Muse

You, perfect distraction.
You, flawless diversion.
Glorious writer's block
in the flesh.
You
are horrible
for my writing.

Never fully versed
in tender language,
I find myself
mining relic heartaches
to reload my pen with.
Until now,
peace only came in pieces so
"shattered"
was the only word
I'd ever learned
synonyms for.

Pain and pen
were playmates.
Tears developed familiar routes
from eyelash to blank page.
Scared, Hurt, and Angry
were my muses,

and the poems
liked that
just fine.

See, I had lonely
down to a science.
Love was a germophobe, and
I was a petri-dish of bacteria.

Depressive diatribes
were totally my wheelhouse.
Break up poems
wrote themselves.
I could cry the blues
like jeans bleeding on
a rinse-cycle.

These days,
life is tie dye bright.
Brilliant and almost hypnotic.
Formless and free.
Now when colors bleed
they just create flashes
of new color.
...and while you're teaching me
to speak rainbow,
I don't know it well enough
to write its hieroglyphs.
Lucky for me
you speak fluent emoji.

Jorge Mendez

Now a days
the pen doesn't move
quite like it used to,
but my soul freestyles
a fresh set of bars
to the rhythm of your walk
every time you step
into a room.

Pain doesn't decorate the page,
but I've doubled over,
sides split,
belly hurting good
from laughter that runs carefree
outside the lines
just like it ought to.

The ink no longer cries rivers,
but I'm learning to draw bridges
connecting you to me,
using old tears
to mix new watercolors.

I've traded
notebook for canvas,
pen for brush,
poem for painting with
a fresh palette of new colors
to create for you with.

I'm sketching dirt paths
into our forever
so that you can help
me pave them,
break out the sidewalk chalk
and decorate them
until the rain plays eraser
and turns them into
neapolitan pools.

My Love,
I'd seen technicolor
from a distance,
but never tasted so many hues
until you...

You
are absolutely horrible…
…for my writing,
but if a picture's worth a thousand words
then I'll paint a thousand pictures,
and keep searching for the right words
while the paint dries.

Jorge Mendez

A Brief List of Things I Know

I bet you've wondered
what's taken me so long
to write a poem for you.

After all this time,
I've honestly wondered myself
and the truth is:
I don't know.
I don't know much of anything.

As a matter of fact,
you could just about
squeeze all the things
I don't know
into the Grand Canyon,
but I've developed
a tight grip
for holding close
the things I do know,
and I've been taking
down some notes:

1.
You're much smarter than me.
Seriously,
you do calculus for fun.
I still count on my fingers,

but I know that
You plus me equals happy.
No matter how many times
you scribble on a white board
you will never formulate the equation
balanced enough
to calculate the depths of
what I feel for you.

2.
We don't always laugh at the same things.

We don't share
the same comedic sensibilities,
but that hasn't stopped me from
learning the levels of your laughter.

From giggles
that sound like the ocean
playing footsies with the shoreline,
and that villainous snicker of sarcasm,
to those from the gut, teary-eyed,
'til your sides split, deep from the belly uproars
that conjure up
all the best parts of me.

Love,
I've even memorized
the cadence of your chuckle.

Jorge Mendez

3.
You possess an affinity for piglets
unlike anything I've ever seen.

4.
Smiles,
can sometimes be heard out loud

and yours
sounds like calm.
Sounds like peace.
Sounds like love in the 60s.
Sounds like Flower Power.

5.
Love,
will give you what you need
even against your will.

Even,
when you don't know
It's what you need.

Especially,
when you don't know
It's what you need.

6.
One can travel the same path
more than once,
differently each time.

Sidewalks can confess
the stories behind their cracks
or cover them with chalk tattoos.
Pretty pastel paths
will lead you anywhere
and everywhere
you can imagine
so, believe me when I tell you,
you can stop counting
the footsteps now.

We don't need to know where
they're taking us,
but we can take notes
along the way.

Jorge Mendez

Semi-Broken Things

Have you ever had something that wasn't necessarily broken, but it didn't work exactly as it was intended to? For example, I had a '90 Geo Prism that wouldn't just start like a normal car. For some reason, I had to turn the key, turn it back, then turn it once more to start it. I also had a toaster that only toasted one side of the bread at a time, so I had to flip it around halfway through to get it fully toasted. The struggle was real back then, but that's not what this is about.

So anyway, I was the only one who knew the trick to start my car. One time, I tried to let a friend borrow it. I taught him the trick, but he never quite got the hang of it and had a hard time. He said, "no one besides you will ever be able to drive this car." I never did get the ignition fixed or even looked at, and eventually the car just up and stopped working all together. (So did the toaster.)

***

I learned a long time ago that I'm kind of like that semi-broken thing we all have. Only thing is, I have no trick that'll "get me started " so to speak. Some days the depression and anxiety make it so I can barely turn the key at all. No matter how much back and forth I put into the key turn, I just don't "start". That's the nature of a semi broken thing. It kind of only works when it wants to and there were many, many days when I didn't "work" at all. More horrible still was the idea that I may never find someone who knew how to "turn the key" for me. Someone who knew the "trick", and that eventually I would just stop "working" altogether.

Then came my wife, Sarah. My partner in this crazy, cosmic, trip through existence on this floating, big, blue ball. Like some sort of emotional mechanic, she manages to get me working nine times out of ten. She makes repairs, but she doesn't fix me. She knows that's not her job or responsibility, but she knows how to turn the key. She knows how to get me started so I can continue fixing myself.

Moreover, she knows that some days it's too rainy to work on the car. Some days even she won't be able to turn the key. Some days I'm just not up for maintenance or repairs. On those days she understands the importance of letting me sit in the driveway. She understands that sometimes you've just got to let it hurt. Sometimes you've just got to sit there and be broken. She understands, that is the nature of a semi-broken thing. On those days she lets me break, but she never lets me too far from the tools.

Jorge Mendez

THE QUIET ONE

... It's been said,
"He thinks too much."
He's never understood what that means.

Jorge Mendez

Dear Silence

Dear silence,

Sometimes,
you're a whisper.
Sometimes,
you're a scream.
Sometimes,
you're so loud,
I can't tell the difference
between
the hammer
and the nail.

Sometimes,
I can barely
hear you
over the sound of
yourself, but
enough!
I hear you.
You've made yourself
loud and clear.

Forgive me,
it wasn't my intention
to drown you out.
It's just,

I'm rarely comfortable
in your presence.
Anxious.
Constantly
search for ways to
break you.
I've been deafening!
I'm sorry.
I've just recently
come to understand
your nature.
The comfort
of your quiet.
The hush
of your contentment.
I've finally grown to
relish reticence.
I acquiesce into
your whisper.

I dissolve into a pause.

Jorge Mendez

Shadow

He must get so tired
of me dragging him around with me
everywhere I go,
keeping him in the dark,
utterly ignoring him.

I'm sure he's sick of hiding behind me.
Never getting any shine,
practically invisible.

He wants the spotlight, but
he doesn't understand,
the lights can be deadly.
He doesn't understand,
that he also can't exist
without them.
He doesn't understand
why he disappears
when the lights ago out.

He doesn't understand because
He thinks I'm the shadow.

Decals

They ask about me.
I tell his stories
but honestly,
I'm mostly just
relic graffiti on the wall.
Decals on the chassis.
Paint on the shell,
chipping.
I am not
the museum.
Merely,
the art in one of its
forgotten exhibits.
I used to feel
fresh.
Fiery.
I'm less important
these days.
As I fade,
he finds himself more
concerned with how
the gears turn,
how hearts sound, and
how far his arms reach.

Jorge Mendez

On the Bone

I can tell
from the debris
in your mane
you're no stranger
to ferocity.

The pulpy pieces
of melancholy
stubbornly lodged
between your teeth
echo of feeding frenzy.

I witnessed
beasts with scars
that match your claws.
The calling card of your brutality.

Afterthoughts
turned aftertaste,
bitter on your pallet.
Insatiable.
Gluttonous.
Quenchless.
Swallowing the chunks whole.
Belly bloated to belligerence.

Predator,
when will you learn?
Not all you devour
will feed you.

Some meat,
is better left on the bone.

Jorge Mendez

Predator and Prey

WITH APOLOGIES TO MY PREY

Forgive me.

I act only out of instinct.
I take no pleasure
in the decimation
of your flesh
beneath my claws.
Your throat
between my teeth
is no trophy.
Your meat
digesting in my belly
does not satisfy.
You taste terrible.
I am no savage.
This is but survival.

Do you understand?

THE PREY'S RESPONSE:

It's alright.
Honest.
I was done here anyway.

Extinction Level Neo-Genesis

Is this the end
or the beginning?
Extinction level event
or
Neo-genesis?
We stand
at the dawn of
the final frontier.
In a staring contest
with Apocalypse.
Where one thing
ends
another begins.
The finish line
starts here.
Death of an era?
Birth of a new age?
Where one thing
ends
another begins.
The finish line
starts here.
We stand
at the dawn of
the final frontier.
In a staring contest
with Apocalypse.

Jorge Mendez

Extinction level event
or
Neo-genesis?
Is this the end
or the beginning?

Lines

Draw them in the sand.

Perforated
Dotted
Fault

On
Off
Land

Out
Under

Pipe
Guide
Border

Front
Stream
Time

Base
Sky
Plot
Under

Jorge Mendez

Neck
Jaw
Head

Laugh
Frown

Flat
Dead
Life

Finish
Cross it.

The Growl

They take me
for granted, you know?
Gluttonous.
Greedy.
Grotesquely wasteful.
80 billion
annual pounds
just
    fucking
        wasted.

Fodder for landfills.
Hog farm feed.
All the while
millions of them starve.

    They starve!

I've heard the howl
of hunger pains.
Seen how it releases
their inner beasts.
I've witnessed them
commit atrocities just
to ease the growl.
They've killed over me
during my abundance.

Jorge Mendez

Imagine them during my scarcity.
Hunger
can motivate
horrible evils.
I've seen it.
Humans are scary
when they're scared.
Villainous.
Imagine what
monstrosities
will be birthed
by my disappearance.
What will fill
the hole
when there's
nothing left of me?

How will they
ease the growl
once I'm gone?

Autumn Stew

Autumn waits
patiently at the doorstep
blending colors in the treetops
to pass the time.

On this side of the door
serenity simmers
on the front burner.
Broth of nature
beckons for my belly,
steam seasons the air,
and a generous ladle
fills my bowl with comfort.

One spoon
thaws the October
from my bones.

I feel my colors changing.

Outside,
Autumn serves a meal
of its own.

Jorge Mendez

Luna

I snuck out
in the middle of the night
to meet with her.
Humming high,
glowing low,
hanging calmly
in the crisp chill
of 3 a.m.

She waited for me there
above the silhouetted tree line,
patiently bouncing beams
against the lake top
to pass the time.

I came to rest beneath her
upon the corpse of a redwood,
reflected my existence
in her pale comfort
safe within the blue ring
of her embrace,
and whispered to her
of my desires
to return home.

Back into the mystic dust of the cosmos,
devolved into something simpler.

Something void of complexity.
A running total
of all the things I am not.
A whole somehow lesser
than the sum of its parts.
A thought
before its conception.

I confided in her
my fears of morning
and the truths it holds,
the prisms it shatters,
the colors it creates, and
the shadows it casts.
What horrid truths could
lie within the clarity
of sun rays?
What angst is born
from the nag of
Mid-day heat?
Where does the darkness hide
once evening yields to dawn?

I begged her to call me home.
To help me steal away
under the cover of night.
A refugee among the stars
with a nap sack full
of defeat and unclaimed victory.
Allow me safe passage into obscurity

Jorge Mendez

under the guise of twilight,
take me home!

…but she refused.
Again.
She just stepped aside,
and left standing there
waiting for the sun.

Soul of August

The soul of August
anoints your brow with salt,
bathes you
in perspiration,
and calls it
baptism.

Heat
doesn't wave,
it disrespects
personal bubbles.
Puts its arm
around you.
Breathes
on you
when it talks.

Clothing clings
like plastic wrap.
Like it's needy.
Wet and weighted
peels away from flesh
like shed skin.
With reluctance.

Humidity
humbles lungs.
It suffocates.

Jorge Mendez

Smothers.
Fits you with
cinder block slippers.
Tethers
your footsteps.
It burdens.

The Sun,
a succubus.
Drains.
It depletes.
It expires you
under the
slow
labored
drip
of Summer...

...and an
ice cream cone
dies
on the
sidewalk.

Rockface

The soil is always
most fragile
at the cliff's edge.

The boldest bluffs
can become confetti
under the weight
of a misstep.

The most massive
of mountains
can devolve into mole hills
of immorality.

Rubble and remorse
crumble from the rockface,
they belong to gravity now
and we've reached
terminal velocity.

Jorge Mendez

Alphabet Soup

All at once the alarms alerted.
Billows of brown smoke
caressed the crying clouds,
distressing the demigods.
Each and every one elevated beyond elation.

Funny how we found freedom
gutturally gurgling,
hell bent and helpless,
ignorantly imitating idiocy
as justice turned jester.

Kill the king.
Let loose the laughter.
Murder miles long madness and malaise.
Note the nuance of nobility.
Open every orifice to
accept the oracle trough osmosis.

Pick a place to puncture.
Quick while it's still quiet, quench the quill.
Relinquish the restless remembering,
the sounds of silent screaming,
temper tantrums, and tunnel vision tear drops.

Understand the upper crust
underestimates your vision.

You are valiant, valuable, vibrating
in a world, war-ridden,
wrecked and worrisome.
Dear warrior,

The experience is the exodus.
Your youthful yearning yields to
your zealous zeitgeist.

Jorge Mendez

Crescendo

The hiss of kettle
as it rolls it over,

                                        Simmering.

The bellow of Earth
moments before it
quakes,

                                        Brooding.

The agony of brakes
fighting freight train
momentum,

                                        Screeching.

The demolition
of what's built
as it collapses,

                                        Surrendering.

The tears
of crystal
as it fractures,

                                        Sobbing.

The hush of
broom bristles
as they clean up,

                                        Repairing.

The laughter
of hammer
as it works,
                                        Rebuilding.

The echo
of love
as it takes a breath,
                                        Persevering.

Jorge Mendez

Neon Bus Stop

The neon flickers
in spastic indecision
casting stuttered shadows
on the figure
waiting below.

The cherry
on the cigarette
glows out loud
then shyly dims
with each drag
reflecting off
the mirrored surface
of damp asphalt.

The exhalation
marries tobacco smoke and fog
until it's hard to tell
where one cloud ends
and the other begins.
Theirs is the
only relationship
that exists
on this corner tonight.

Headphones drown out
the voice of yesterday.
The one whispering, "Stay".

The promise of "tomorrow"
somehow less seductive than
a pocket full of "goodbye" or
the allure of "right now".

                Either to
                or from something
                we're all running.

The bus
sleepwalks
through the city
cycling through passengers
like dream states.

The labored breath of air brakes
breaks the silence.
It's tires,
though tired
don't complain.
They just carry on
like overnight bags
small enough
to hold an entire lifetime.

Last stop before
head hits pillow.
Its doors yawn
with invitation.

My Imaginary Friends

Jorge Mendez

> Either to
> or from something
> we're all running.

The light
calling from inside,
fluorescent and harsh,
kind of reminds you
of tough love.
Kind of sounds
like it just said,
"Well, come on if you're coming."

The cherry dies
hissing on the sidewalk
as tobacco smoke
kisses fog one last time.

The figure
accepts the invitation.
The neon still
can't make up its mind
flinching in the
farewell of taillights.

> Either to
> or from something
> we're all running
> and it's been a really, really, long night.

The City Breathes in Technicolor

The city breathes
in technicolor.

It's pulse
massaging my fingertips.
Vibrant and energetic
like primaries.
Subtle like secondaries.
Calm like neutrals.
Easy as earth tones.

The colors bleed
but don't smear,
don't smudge.
They rainbow together.

Rubix Cube.
Every corner,
every block,
a new hue to the cube.

The city breathes
In technicolor

It bleeds
in shades of gray.

Jorge Mendez

Gray

With a sip of Earl,
I become reserved. Calm.
The clouds roll in.
Subdued.
Resolute.
Impartial.
My memory an elephant.
A cross breed of two neutrals.
Neither dark nor bright.
Unpolished,
never to feel the
luster of silver.
Only the frailty
of ash and cinder.
The mass between my ears
aches with indecision,
while the earworm sings
"Stuck in the Middle with You."
The sky yawns in boredom.
Pours itself
onto the sidewalk
with indifference.
Age doesn't wash away.
We are neither right nor wrong,
but the tombstones
beg to differ.

Astro-Aquarian

Walk along the shoreline of the universe.
Stand at the edge of the galaxy.
Feel the stars between your toes.
Let the comets lazily lap waves over your feet.

Take a dip in the cosmos.
Rise against the gravity of tide.
Swim through a planet's rings.
Backstroke through blackholes.

Somewhere between
The Crab and Twin Fishes
a leviathan lurks,
but fear not the murky depths.
Embrace the expanse.
The vastness.
Become comfortable
with the miniscule.

It all begins with an explosion.

Somewhere
in the Slick Abyss
a starfish goes supernova,
each arm
reaching for new life.

Jorge Mendez

THE JESTER

*... Laughs much too late.
Doesn't seem to take
anything seriously...*

Jorge Mendez

Nemesis

The alarm clock
has no bedside manner.
Rude and callous.
Rings like rapture.

Dead arm
searching in the dark,
swinging blindly at
my tormentor.
He remains unphased
by my attempt
at a defense.

It simply slinks away
and attacks 10 min later.
This time louder.
This time longer.
This time angry.

He yells,
THIS DAY WILL START WITH OUT YOU!

RISE UP!!!!

or get left behind.

A Letter from Igloo

Attention Human Caregiving Units,

This correspondence serves to inform you of some provisions and conditions I feel could improve.
Firstly, the greens you so lovingly grew yourself for me to eat are at best, unsatisfactory, as is the astronomically expensive nutritional supplement you prepare for me.
Fresh.
Daily.

Henceforth, I request... Nay. I demand a rotating buffet of tasty insects. I prefer Dubia Roaches as they are easier to catch than crickets. Never mind quieter. You'll enjoy this, I imagine as I've heard you complain incessantly about their chirping on more than just a few occasions. Meal worms are acceptable, though passable is a more appropriate adjective however, horned worms would be most desirable. The significant cost disparity is inconsequential. While on the subject of my feeding, I would like to note that I also do not appreciate the frequency with which I find my meal bowl empty. It seems you simply cannot fulfill even this simplest, most basic of duties. I recommend increasing the size of the bowl or perhaps you could just use that big human brain of yours and just remember to refill it every 5 to 7 minutes.
Lastly, my enclosure is, well...adequate. I understand its easily 3 times larger than my species requires but, I still think we can do better. Maybe something with a balcony and an H.O.A.?
I'm not sure what steps you intend to take to rectify your short comings, but I trust you will engage and react accordingly and with a sense of urgency.

Jorge Mendez

Don't beat yourself up. Just fix it.
I only hold you but so responsible.
After all, you're only human.

Warmest Regards,
Igloo
The Bearded Dragon

Cellular Degeneration

You know just what buttons to push,
how to turn me on,
how to unlock my secrets,
gain access.

I am a gallery on display.
Fix your eyes upon me,
face to face.
You dare not break your gaze,
you're captivated.

Blue toothed smile.
Face glowing from the light of mine.
Your eyes hungrily
taking me in.
I just love how you get lost in me.

Cradle me.
Absorb me through your palm.
Fingers
tapping,
swiping,
sliding,
clicking,
touching.
I'm more than turned on,
I'm connected.
Synced.

Jorge Mendez

I'm with you always,
firm in your grip.
Alerted.
Notified.
Your navigator riding shotgun on this
information superhighway.
I give you anything you could ask for.
I'm all you could
ever need.
There is you
and there is me
and I possess
the ability
to steal your attention from
anyone in the room.
I'm selfish
because you let me be.

Look at you!
Panicked
when you thought you'd lost me.
Frantic at the thought.
Desperate.
You even begged your friends to
call out to me
while you listened for my voice
forgetting
you had left me
silenced.

You can't function without me.
Leaning on me
even as even as I grow weak.
Draining me
of every ounce of life I have,
and still in my death
you curse me.

I am your drive and your distraction.
Your focus and your folly.
I may be the object,
but you
are the possession.

I own you!
You belong to me!

You may give me power,
but let's be clear.
I am now and forever
the one
who is in
charge.

Jorge Mendez

A Call from Beyond

Hello?
Yes, this is he.
Who am I speaking with?
Don Lewis?
I can't say I know a...
Wait.
You mean,
Don Lewis as in
Carol Baskins' husband
Don Lewis?
You gotta be shittin' me!
I thought you were dead.
Oh, you are?
Huh.
You don't say.
But then how...?
Ok, I'm listening.
What?
What the fuck?
No fucking way man.
What do you mean,
She fed you to a tiger?
Like a tiger, tiger?
Shut the fuck up!
Gahdamn!
That shit's crazy.
Ok,
so, what should I do?
Call who?
Joe Exotic?

WHAT THE FUCK IS A JOE EXOT…
Alright, if you say so.
You too man.
Talk to later Don.
You too.
Yea you too.
Uh huh.
Ok.
Uh huh.
Yea.
Ok.
Ok.
Ok bye.

Jorge Mendez

About Last Night

I've been thinking of you all day.
Remembering the richness of
last nights untouched portions,
the full body of your flavors,
the complexity of your composition,
the beckoning aroma,
how you danced
upon my eager pallet, and your
subtle textures on my tongue.

The workday weans away
and I'm reminded of you
with every billow of my belly.
I hunger for you.
A beast famished for your freshness.
Ravenously craving to devour you
morsel by morsel,
bite by deliberate bite.
Satisfying every layer of
this hunger pain.
I'm starved for you.

When I come home
things are really going to heat up and
once the microwave chimes
you won't stand a chance.

Covert Ops

I wait until they are all asleep.
The cover of darkness,
shield for
my late night mission.

Sneakily,
I creep out of bed,
army crawl
across the floor,
and out the door.

Coast is clear.

With my back
against the wall,
I navigate my way
down the hall
to the staircase.

Now I must
move in total,
calculated silence.
These steps are creaky, and
I can't afford to
give up my position.
Inch by deliberate inch
I slink until I reach

Jorge Mendez

the fourth step from the bottom.
This one is extra loud.
I extend my leg
in a huge arch
leaping over it
and land lightly on the
third from last step.
I barely make the leap,
but I land without a sound
and proceed with
my mission.
Once I reach the bottom
of the stairs,
I do a quick tuck and roll
and dodge the
sensor in the foyer.

Almost there.

I can see the dim glow
of the nightlight from here.
I make my way stealthily
toward it.
I tiptoe around the corner and
Boom!
I'm in!

I slowly open the refrigerator door
being careful not to
make too much noise.

Blinded by the light,
I find the leftover pie.
Slyly, I peel back
the aluminum foil cover.
With all the
composure I can muster,
I pull a fork from the drawer
and dig in.

Mission Accomplished!

Jorge Mendez

Fungus

Lotus on the couch.
The ground looks miles away.
I could sky dive forever
from this cliffside
into the kaleidoscope ocean,
backstroke through
the swirling kite ribbons.
The sky
is my swimming pool.

These stones
turn cotton candy in my mouth.
Every crevice,
every chip,
every sharp edge
dissolves soft
against my tongue.
The grass blades
grow tree trunk tall while
ant hills Everest.

Someone sings about
a Ferris Wheel and classic rock.

Back against the wall of the Gravitron.
Orbs carousel,
the lights
bleed into hula hoops.

I'm hungry.
Everything tastes like dreams.

I sweat a reservoir.
I drink a water park.

I breathe like moonbeams.
I sleep like silence.

Jorge Mendez

Tommy Boy

Tommy Boy,
Your acting makes me wanna keep my
'Eyes Wide Shut'.
Being so wildly over-rated is
'Risky Business'
when you're convinced you're a
'Top Gun',
but you're actually
'Shattered Glass'.
You're no
'Legend'.
You just chase
'Knight and Day',
hopping on Oprah's couch like it's
'The Edge of Tomorrow'
Screaming "show me the money",
bleeding the junket dry
like you just had an
'Interview with the Vampire'.
You're really bad
in good movies.
It frustrates me to
'Oblivion'
how you need
'A Few Good Men'
in the edit room
to pull off a

'Mission Impossible'
and make you look like
A Maverick with
'All the Right Moves'
when you're actually more of a
'Rain Man'.
You're barely
'Collateral'
for
'The Color of Money'.

I'm sorry Tommy,
I just don't like you.
I don't have a reason.
I said what I said.
...but,
I liked you in
'Tropic Thunder'.
I don't care.

Jorge Mendez

Retail Employee's Holiday Prayer

Now I take me off to work.

I hope the customers aren't jerks,

and if I snap before its thru

I pray it's not my job I lose.

Teddy's New Roommate

For weeks,
I had the crib all to myself.
The cushy pillows,
the plush blanky,
cool-ass galaxy mobile
over my head.
It was friggin' sweet!
Just me,
living my best life
in the once peaceful
tranquility of this empty nursery.
I had everything a teddy bear could need.

Until
the day
they brought
         Her home!
My new roommate.

A 7 pound 2 ounce
bundle of absolute horror.
A doomsday alarm in a cotton candy onesie.
A wicked child with the shrill shriek
of a tortured banshee.
A hell spawn.
Fruit of evil

Jorge Mendez

born of sulfur.
I mean,
a real little shit.

She moved in
and sleep moved out.

Her cry was other worldly.
The type of noise
that cuts through silence
with hostility.
Imagine a mix of
the t-rex from Jurassic Park
and Mariah Carey's falsetto.
A death wail
that hung in the air for hours,
and I had to sit in there with
this demon baby while she screamed
Dark Realm incantations
into the ether, conjured
from the blackest pits of hell.

From that day forward
My sanctuary
was no longer,
and don't even get me started
on the diapers.

Tug, Yank, Tear

Tug.
Yank.
Tear.
Day after day.
For days at a time.

I'm skewered
through my middle,
hung on the wall
of the filthiest
room in the house.

Tug
Yank.
Tear.
Day after day.
For days at a time.

I'm so valuable.
So rare.
Such a commodity,
yet I'm soiled.
Discarded.
Flushed away.

Tug.
Yank.
Tear.

Jorge Mendez

Day after day.
For days at a time.

Until,
there's nothing left of me
but my bare
cardboard
skeleton.

Tug.
Yank.
Tear.

Then I'm replaced
like I never
existed.

Poem's Ad

Block-experiencing writer
Seeking poem to break slump
Must exceed 20 lines
Totaling no less than 4 stanzas
Verses must be unique and flow smoothly
Line breaks must be sharp
Punctuation is key
Meter must be timely but uncontrived
Language elegant and delicate
But commanding and powerful
Rhyming couplets need not apply

757-555-7878

Jorge Mendez

Poem Responds to Ad

I think, I may be
the poem you're looking for.

I am 6 stanzas, 40 lines
of finger snap inducing,
ooh and aah producing
bar divinity.

A soliloquy
of epiphanies
intrinsically precise.
Wit sharp
as the key
of life.
A cry into the night.
A tale of woe.

I am a hybrid haiku.
Winter in a window.
The item not on the menu,
A poem made to order.
Written drunk,
edited sober,
birthed in a cloud
of weed and clover.

I am the cure
to all that ails you.

The lines
you hide behind
that veil you.
The hero
that failed you.

I am the light
in the writing
you cast your shadow with, and
the writer's block
you battle with.

I am
the poem you're looking for,
Your only saving grace.
Your reflection on the page.
Period.
Double space.

Jorge Mendez

THE GIRL

...the advocate.
The voice of reason,
the wailing cry for justice...

Jorge Mendez

Failure

I don't write poems.
I write failed attempts
at finding
the formula
that will save us.

Instructions for Putting Together a Puzzle

1. Break open the box it came in and dump the pieces out. Hold on to the lid with the original image as you'll need it in the future to refer back to.

2. Spread them out in front of you, face up, so you can better see what your pieces look like.

3. Find all the pieces with flat sides. Run your fingers across the smooth, pronounced edges. Learn them. These will form you borders, create your outline, and hold together all the pieces you place inside.

4. Take them all in, notice how each is shaped differently, formless, and abstract. Slowly, one by one begin filling in the pieces that match. Create links and patterns as you begin to see an image forming.

5. When a piece doesn't fit where you think it should, don't force it. Set it aside, come back to it later. Soon it will find its way into the place it belongs.

6. Should you find a piece missing, don't panic. Remember, there is beauty in the incomplete, and not a one of us is whole.

Jorge Mendez

Monster House

One thing
I know without question:

There are monsters
in every corner of this house.

All of them
with their own
bed to hide under.
Each with a closet
they call home.

But I do not
evict them, as
I suspect
I put a few of them there myself.

True Colors

Some people's
true colors
have bled and
smeared so much
they'll match anything.

Jorge Mendez

Purple

Lavender
is bashful.
Shy
like shuttered tulips.

Lilac,
a bit more
bold.

Boysenberry
is stern, serious.

Eggplant,
a friendly jester.

Grape and Plum,
mischievous siblings.

Wisteria
and her sister Heather
dance to the
Electric Indigo.

Iris,
somewhat indignant, watches
from afar.

Violet
calls for the moon
by name,
pulls her into
the twilight.

Amethyst
reigns.

Her majesty,
Royal,
conducts the spectrum.

Jorge Mendez

We All Keep Secrets

Oh child.
We all keep secrets.

I, myself speak coded silence.
A whisper in a megaphone.

I'd tell you,
but it'd kill me so,
listen intently
to the muted.
Look closely
at the invisible.

Everything you need
to know is right there,
hidden in the spaces
between words,
in the pauses
between sentences,
in the quiet seconds
between breaths.

Oh child.
We all keep secrets.

Mostly from ourselves.

Rage Review

Upon my arrival
I originally thought,
wow, what a beautiful place!
Spacious skies,
amber waves of grain,
purple mountains majesty,
fruited plains...
I mean,
just lovely.
I thought, now here's
a place where
truths are self-evident!
But I must say,
It's not quite
the Land of the Opportunity
It's cracked up to be.
Look around.
The infrastructure
and the power grid
are logistical nightmares.
There is somehow
a problem with both
homelessness and abandoned buildings.
Everyone is sick,
but no one can afford medicine.
Police murder unarmed
citizens with reckless impunity.

Jorge Mendez

The educational systems
are outdated and failing.
Equality is all but nonexistent.
There are literally
more guns than people,
and even though there's
a mass shooting
literally every day,
the leadership does
absolutely nothing about it.
There is however,
an overabundance of
thoughts and prayers.
I'm told I could protest
but then my protest gets criticized.
I tried to complain
to the proper authorities,
but was quickly met with,
"If you don't like it
 you can just leave!!!"
How's that for 50-star service?
I expected more from
"The greatest country in the world!"
What a shithole!
America.
Zero out of 10.
Do not recommend.

BLM

If he takes a knee
they want to riot.

If he takes a bullet
they're all quiet.

Seems the act of being black
is enough to make them violent,

and just trying to survive
is noncompliance.

Jorge Mendez

Exit Newtown North

Exit Newtown North.
Approaching the light at
Virginia Beach Boulevard at a snail's pace.
From about eight car lengths in front of me,
I see man limping between the two rows of gas guzzlers
poisoning the only air he has to breathe.

He wore his story around his neck like an albatross.
His clothes were at least 3 sizes too big,
but I imagine that once upon a time
they probably fit him perfectly.
A business jacket from the late nineties
hung sullen over his shoulders,
shirt stained heavily with hunger pains,
pants held up by a frayed extension cord.
A neglected Nike on one foot.
a rejected Reebok on the other.
He moves like it hurts him to.
On his head he wore a scarf
underneath two hats
and from beneath it all,
I could just make out a face.

Flesh heavy,
brown, and dry like abandoned leather,
rough with soil, stubble, and suffering.
Every wrinkle holding tightly within it

a memory of something broken.
Eyes sunken in and dim with
their last fleeting notion of hope,
lips cracked and crimson
like bleeding fire trucks.
Just beyond them,
a shattered incomplete smile
that no one's seen in what must be years.
The creases in his knuckles ache out loud.
Deep like tiny canyons
filled with blood-stained disillusionment.
Rejection has caked itself under his fingernails.
His hands looked defeated,
shakily holding a cardboard sign that read:
"Hungry Please Help"

The tattered mass of him
shuffled past vehicle after vehicle
as windows either remained shut,
or rolled up shamelessly.
Drivers and passengers
turned their heads away from him
as if afraid to come face to face
with their own compassion,
fumbling with $500 cell phones
pretending not to notice him.

The man in the BMW in front of me shoed him away
like an insect he was allergic to.
As though homelessness was contagious.

Jorge Mendez

God forbid the stench of hunger
phantom past your greedy nostrils.
Heaven help you if you reach into
your $50 wallet for a five-dollar bill.
As I'm thinking this, I roll my window down
just in time to hear the homeless man say to him,
"God bless you".

I hand him 3 dollars and 67 cents,
everything I had,
and when my hand met his,
I recognized him.

He looked like my father.
He looked like my brother.
He looked like my nephew, my cousin, my roommate.
He looked like my friend,
he looked like the mailman,
he looked like a doctor,
like a lawyer,
like a store clerk,
like a fire fighter,
he looked like a soldier, like a sailor, like a marine.
He looked like a hero.

He looked like a mechanic,
he looked like a city worker,
he looked like a carpenter, a mason, a plumber, like an electrician.
He looked like a preacher.
He looked like a monk.

He looked like a deacon.
He looked like God!

He looked like someone's son.
Someone's husband.
Someone's dad.

He looked like you…

He looked like...
He looked like
me.

Jorge Mendez

Coming Soon

Have you heard?

We can explore the cosmos with a rocket.
We have computers that'll fit in our pockets.
A disease with no sure way to stop it,
but I'm sure a cure's coming soon.

We have sticks to help us take selfies.
Glutton free bread, to keep us all healthy.
We still haven't answered to "help me",
but I'm sure that's coming soon.

Have you heard?
Have you heard?

We landed a rover on Mars.
We have satellites among the stars.
Still can't heal emotional scars,
but I'm sure that's coming soon.

We've taught robots, how to shoot guns.
We made shoes that can track where you've run.
Still haven't quite mastered the hug,
but I'm sure that's coming soon.

Have you heard?
Have you heard?

Have you heard?
Have you heard?

We have earphones to help us not listen.
Contact lenses all colors, no vision.
Can't stop fighting over gods and religion,
but I "pray" that's coming soon.

There's mothers stricken with grief.
Cities that fear the police.
No clear sign we will find peace,
but I hope it's coming soon.

We can create a world that rejoices,
if we learn from the ills of our choices.
They haven't yet stolen our voices,
but I bet that's coming soon.

Jorge Mendez

On Fire

Make no mistake.
Despite it being 3/4 water,
the Earth is,
in fact, burning.

The flames came as
no surprise.
The embers had been
threatening to billow
for some time.
Glowing.
Hissing.
Warning us.
It's not like we didn't notice
how hot it had become.
It was trial by fire.
Some of us
fought the inferno until
the extinguishers grew exhausted,
some fanned the flames,
others roasted marshmallows.

Man perhaps,
would have been better off,
had we never discovered fire.

Cockroach

Fun Fact:

A cockroach
can live for up to a week
after it's been decapitated
because its brain
does not control its breathing, and
blood doesn't carry oxygen
throughout its body
like a human's does.

Eventually,
the cockroach will die
of starvation
since the one thing it actually
needs its head for
is to eat.

I say all that to say,
when we start
to eat the rich,
don't be alarmed
if they're still moving.

Jorge Mendez

The Price

…and away like limbs
of a leper
fell the chunks
of justice.

From the dust and rubble,
from the ash and burnt Earth
we collected any surviving
portions of peace and
offered them up
to the last of us,
as equally
as math allows.

One cried out,
"Mine has blood on it!"

The response came,
"They all do!"

"They all do."

Misunderstood Mountain

I do not
fear the end.

I do not
tremble at the treble
in songs of Revelations.

The rumble of trumpets
does not disrupt me.

I'm well aware
the self
is rarely itself
until its torn open
at its seam.
Raw.
Bare.
Bloody and erupting
like lava from
the mouth of
a misunderstood mountain.

Truth falls like
confetti from the rock face,
and it's just as big
a pain to clean up.

Jorge Mendez

I heard them yelling,
"Burn it down!"

It's always hottest
when the lights
shine brightest.

Most of us
can't stand the heat,
and none of us were
ever really that cool.

66 Questions for God

Hey God,
What's up?

Do You have a minute?
Mind if I ask you a few questions?
How about we start at the beginning?

Like, how exactly did you create day and night
on the first day, but the sun moon and stars on day four?
Since Adam and Eve didn't know right from wrong until
eating from the tree of knowledge of good and evil,
why did you punish them for something
they didn't yet understand?

And if you know all
then you knew they would be tempted,
so why allow Satan so close to your innocent creations
and just look on while he led Eve into temptation?

Why don't you heal amputees?

If you make us all, and made some of us gay, then
why send gays to hell for being how you made them?
Besides, if we're all made in your image,
doesn't that make you a little gay?

When two teams pray to win the championship,
how do you pick which team's prayer to answer?

Jorge Mendez

Do you flip a coin?

Why is the Heimlich maneuver more effective
on choking victims than prayer is?
Why did you give us medicine if prayer heals all illness?
If you know our fate, why even bother with prayer?
It's like praying for a book you've already read to have a different ending.

Why did you create venomous creatures?
Which one was your favorite dinosaur?
Did you kill them off because they didn't believe in you?
Why didn't you mention them in the bible?
and while we're on that subject,
if the bible is truly your word,
and you're perfect,
why are there so many contradictions in it?

Why would you write an
instruction manual
then make it open to interpretation?

If it's so important for us to get your message,
why make your message so difficult to understand?
Didn't you proofread the bible?
…or was it the Koran?
In 1 Samuel 15:11 you say you regret making Saul king.
Doesn't that then mean that you do make mistakes and are not, in fact, perfect?

...and if you know all,
how didn't you know you would eventually regret
making him king in the first place?

How did taking your name in vain and worshipping false idols
make it to your top ten things to never, ever do,
but slavery and rape somehow managed to slip your mind?

How many donkeys did Jesus ride into Jerusalem?
Was it one like Mark, Luke, and John said, or was it two like
Matthew said?
Was Jesus crucified on the first day of Passover
like the gospel of John says,
or on the second day like the other three gospels say?
I'm only asking because both versions are in your
"perfectly infallible" book.
Why couldn't you forgive us for our sins
without sacrificing your son?
And if you resurrected him three days later
how is that even really a sacrifice?
In Deuteronomy 23:2 you say,
"No one of illegitimate birth
shall enter the assembly of the LORD;
none of his descendants,
even to the tenth generation,
shall enter the assembly of the LORD."
So, why didn't that rule apply to your son Jesus?
I mean, it's not like you married Mary, right?

Jorge Mendez

The duck billed platypus.
Seriously,
what the fuck?

What's your beef with third world countries?
Why don't they get enough water?
Do you have a hard time
hearing their prayers
over the growling bellies?
How do you decide which children to starve and not starve?

Do you flip a coin?

Why do you need us to worship you?
Why do you demand we idolize you?
Why do you need us to believe in you?
Are you really that insecure?
Why do you punish those who don't?
Hitler believed in you, is he in heaven?
Did you send Gandhi to hell?

Speaking of hell,
how can you offer unconditional love and
threaten eternal damnation all in one breath?
How was drowning damn near every living thing on the planet
an act of love?
Why did you place conditions on your unconditional love?
How can I enjoy heaven if someone I love is burning in hell?

If you know what's in our hearts,
why ask Abraham to kill his son to prove he loved you?
Why gamble with Satan over the life of Job just to prove a point?
Sure, you gave him new livestock, a new wife and new kids,
but was that supposed to make him forget about
the family he lost in your little wager with the devil?
Why create the devil?
Do you need him?
Is he the Joker to your Batman?
or the Hyde to your Jekyll?

Why have you allowed so many to literally get away with murder?
Why have you let so many pay for crimes they didn't commit?
Why do you give some babies birth defects?
When creating natural disasters,
how do you decide which land masses and people to obliterate?

DO YOU FLIP A COIN?

Why have you allowed hurt,
allowed thirst,
allowed famine,
disease,
poverty,
pollution,
rape,
murder,
slavery,
sex trafficking,

Jorge Mendez

child abuse,
senseless death,
violence,
and countless wars in your name?

Why have you allowed
so much
suffering
for so,
so long?

Why?

When I was a child,
my sister and I
fought constantly.
My mother
separated us
to keep us from hurting ourselves.

God,
We're down here
killing one another.

What are you waiting for?
Are we not your children?

Haven't you heard us?
We've been praying for you
to do something,
for a very,
very long time.

Jorge Mendez

Human Deities

...And she wondered
if the Gods
were uncomfortable
crammed into
the spaces between galaxies.
Shoulder to shoulder
like souls on busy subways,
irritated to the point
of suffocation.

...wondered
if their arrogance
could just about
eclipse the sun
the way her palm does
when she holds it up
to the sky,
if the universe expanded
to accommodate
their egos...

What demons could
a deity have to hide?
Were the cosmos
a big enough closet
for their skeletons?
Are they haunted by

the spirits of regret?
Do their insecurities
eat at their divinity?
Do they ever smile to
hide their hurt?

And if so,

Do they know
just how human that makes them?

Jorge Mendez

Broadcasting

Signal weak.
Attempting to dial
into your frequency.
Drunk off
the static
between your stations.

Tales from a
telescopic antenna,
our amplitude modulated.

Gasping for oxygen
over the airwaves.

It's become clear,
just because
you tune in
doesn't mean
you're picking up a signal.

Some of us
just don't transmit
at the same frequency,
and some of us
aren't even
broadcasting at all.

Somedays

Somedays
get so heavy,
I feel like my
soul gained weight.

Somedays
ache like
shoeless feet marching
through gravel.

Somedays
get too hard to bear.
Too painful to stomach.
Too ugly to look at.
Too dark to see through.

Somedays,
it's just impossible
to push away the awful.

Somedays,
I feel it's just
not worth it anymore.

But not today.

Jorge Mendez

THE CHILD

... my favorite.
Sings out of key.
Doesn't care.
Just Sings louder...

Jorge Mendez

Curfew Was a Streetlight

When I was a child
I,
was powerful!

I possessed
the ability
to transform the
vacant lots of our neighborhood
into magical lands.

A stick
could cast a spell.
A branch
could ward off trolls.
A paper towel roll
was a pocket telescope,
or a horn,
or a dagger,
and a cardboard box
had limitless potential.

With but a thought,
I could turn it from a fort,
to a rocket,
to a pirate ship,
then back into a fort

faster than you could
wield an empty gift wrap tube sword.

Grass stains
were spoils of war.
A scab
was a badge of honor;
ammunition
was made of foam.

Stress
was the inability
to start your game
no matter how many times
you blew into
the cartridge.
Memory was just
something we lost
as we got older,
and calling a time-out
was how we saved
game progress.

Programs came on television,
applications were
for finding jobs,
and catching a virus
just meant you
couldn't play for a few days.

Jorge Mendez

A mother's voice
was a dinner bell.

Curfew was a Streetlight.

I drank water from
a garden hose
and lived to tell the story.

Caterpillars

The caterpillar
does not know
it will be a butterfly.
It weaves it's cocoon
simply because it's heart
says so.

The butterfly
cannot remember
being a caterpillar.
It just knows
it is now beautiful.

The abandoned chrysalis
does not know
all the work it has done.
It simply knows
it is now exhausted.

The child chasing
fluttery wings
knows nothing of this science.
They only know
that they are happy
because their heart
says so.

Jorge Mendez

Endangered Species

I saw a video
of a cat snuggling
a dolphin,
and I couldn't help
but wonder
why differences
matter so much to people?

How is it beasts
display more
humanity than
humans do?

Perhaps,
we're the animals?

Perhaps,
we are endangered?

Perhaps,
that's for the best?

Life Saver

Back when Gina still loved Martin
and Fresh Prince was still in college,
back when Pippen was still ballin',
I was going all in.
Writing rhymes in the kitchen;
beating on the table spittin'.
Mama would get so pissed,
"cut the racket, wash the dishes",
but mama just didn't get it.
I get it,
it just wasn't for her.
I tried to play her my albums,
she couldn't make out the words.
To her it sounded absurd,
just a bunch of bass and talking,
but hip hop had grabbed a hold of her son
and she couldn't stop it.
So instead, she bought
me notebooks and pencils
to flex my mental.
Tools to help me succeed
and realize all my dreams.

It seems
like a lifetime ago.
Funny how life can go so slow
yet fly by

Jorge Mendez

in the wink of an eye.
The passage of time
scatters across the written page
as pain and emotion
waste away,
nights turn into days,
and poems carry away
malaise.

I wonder if Mama knew
the things that her son would do,
the things I was working through,
the emotional black and blues?
The hurt that I felt in private?
The tears I cried in silence?
The thoughts of anger and violence
that I spilled into those pages?

Or how the written word
saved my life
on many a sleepless night,
or how I wouldn't even be here
had I never learned to write?

Orphans

What becomes
of orphaned lines
abandoned on random
scraps of paper?

The forgotten parables
scribbled onto fragile napkins,
the neglected couplets
crammed into the narrow margins
of dusty periodicals?

The bones of work,
never given flesh,
left to wither
in the catacombs
of dresser drawers,
and the unmarked pocket tombs
of old winter coats?
Where do they go?

I imagine,
that most,
weak and without substance,
do indeed die off.
Embarrassments made illegible carcasses.
Unceremoniously scratched out
beneath a merciless

Jorge Mendez

ink blob onslaught,
decidedly decimating
any trace of its conception.

Others
of course,
do eventually get adopted
by families they verse well with.
They fall into the fold,
develop meter,
and roll off the tongue.

…but the rarest of them,
the most stubborn,
they leave stains.
They grow legs.
They fend for themselves.
They stand
well enough alone.
Hieroglyphics
from the walls of
a subconscious.
Primitive imprints
from a thought's
oldest ancestor.
Scrawlings of psyche
that offer a sliver of
insight into creation
at its most instinctual.

The honest ones,
they take root,
they impact soul,
move spirit,
and grant
immortality.

Jorge Mendez

Just

I spent the first
12 years of my life
trying to be just
like you.

I've spent the
rest of it
just trying to
like you.

Both are failures
I do not regret.

Play Date

My demons
want a play date,

but the last time
they came over
they broke all my toys,
destroyed
the building block castle
I usually hide in,
left my room a mess
that I had to clean up
all by myself

and honestly,
mostly,
I'm just not up for company.

Jorge Mendez

Recess

Empty tire
rocks lazy in
the breeze of reverie.

Swing sets
murmur
fragmented messages and
muffled memories
as they pendulum past
each other.

See-saws
keep time
like the metronome
of my childhood,
teetering on the edge
of repression.

Daydreams dangle
from barbed
monkey bars
over a quicksand box
ready to swallow up
innocence.

Only one way down
from the top
of the slide, and
this playground
holds more danger
than delight.

Jorge Mendez

To the Dreams I Can't Remember

To the dreams I can't remember:

It's no one's fault.
Some things are
better forgotten.

Left faint and foggy
in the dusty
photo albums
of subconscious.

That's how you kill
a nightmare.

      You know?
      They say,
      "The devil's in the details."

I'm sure
you were
unmemorable,

only for my own
protection.

Galactose

Far from the
Red-Hot bitterness
of this planet.
Beyond the crimson
Cherry Cordial we call Mars.
Further than the reaches
of the Milky Way.
Nestled between the
Star Crunch Nebula and
The Goo-Goo Cluster Asteroid Field
there exists a saccharine planet.
A confectionery world to rival even the great
Wonka's Chocolate Factory!
A planet the
Nerds and Smarties call
Galactose 6-12-6.
I know
you're probably thinking
I'm some sort of
Air Head or a Goober,
but I assure you
its real.
I've seen it.
My shuttle
peeled through the
outer candy shell atmosphere
like an Atomic Fire Ball!

Jorge Mendez

My decent continued
spiraling through
Cotton Candy cumulonimbus
by light of Marshmallow Moon
careening out of control
over the Sno-Cap Mountains.
Finally, crash landing with a Crunch
onto the Rock Candy banks
of Butterscotch River.
Through the amber hue,
I could see it was
teeming with Swedish Fish.
All around me the air
smelled of creme filled pastries
and powdered donuts.
I barely got a chance to
take it all in before I found myself
face to face with an
angry mama Gummi Bear.
I took off running through a lollipop forest.
Bounding over Bon-Bon bushes
and leaping broken limbs
from licorice trees.
I finally lost the Gummi Bear
and came across a field of
Jellybean crops.
There I met a Jolly Rancher
named Milton and his
Sour Patch Kids,
Mike & Ike.

I asked him for help with my ship,
and he agreed, but wanted me to
stay for dinner first.
He fixed us a hardy meal of
Circus Peanuts and Lemon Heads.
I did not enjoy it, but did not want to be rude.
Afterwards we found our way to my ship.
He said "we better hurry, looks like its gonna sprinkle"
All of a sudden, actual sprinkles
in every color began raining from the sky.
It only lasted for a moment
then a Skittles Rainbow
arched across the sugary heavens.
A few pieces of
Bubble Tape later and
my ship was ready.
"You're a Life Saver!", I said.
"No.", he replied with a Snicker,
"I'm a Jolly Rancher."
I told him I'd send him
100 Grand on Payday,
then blasted off like a Starburst.

Now how's that for a Whopper!?

Jorge Mendez

The Previews

The smell of
buttered popcorn
beckons me from just
beyond the
box office.
I'm here early
with my pre-purchased ticket
waiting in line
to overpay
for this evening's snacks.
A medium bucket of
heavily buttered popcorn,
a large fruit punch light ice
(I always ask for light ice otherwise
I'm not having fruit punch with ice
I'm having ice with fruit punch,
nobody wants that),
and a box of Reese's Pieces.
Grand Total:
$803.78
Hmmm?!?
She must have Forgotten
to ring up my drink.
Score!

I'm here early.
There's just me and an usher

who's looking at me wondering,
"why's this jackass so early?"
as he half heartedly
sweeps up the
foot trampled popcorn
and candy wrappers
left over from the last showing.

I have my choice of seats.
Back Row.
Way at the top.
Dead center.
Perfect.
The seat beside me
holds my tray of
cinematic munchies.

One by one,
 I correctly answer
every movie trivia question
flashed on screen.
I feel quite accomplished
though I shouldn't
since the questions
weren't hard at all.

I expect the room to
start filling up soon
and that my snack tray
may have to give up its seat,

Jorge Mendez

but it doesn't.
No one sits in my row at all.
As a matter of fact,
there's only a handful
of people in here besides me.
Excellent!
I hate crowded theatres.

Soon the lights dim
and the previews start.
This is my favorite part.
This is why
I'm here early.
I hate missing the previews.

Movie trailers are like
a glimpse into the future,
a foretelling of what you will see,
a promise of good things to come.
I think we all love the previews.
I mean,
who doesn't
need something
to look forward to?

The Seed

The
seed
selflessly
volunteers.
It
cracks
itself
open.
Buries
it's
carcass
then
resurrects
itself
bringing
new
life.
Baring
fruit.
This
is
the
nature
of
generosity.
To
give

Jorge Mendez

without
reward.
To
take
root
in
that
which
is
good.

Sparrow

Sweet sparrow.

The sun awakes
feeling refreshed
this morning.
The air is
crisp,
sharp,
eager.

You have
an entire sky
to explore.
Clouds to find
your shape in.

Introduce
yourself
to your reflection
in a drop of dew.
Today
you meet
your truest self.

Tip toe to the edge
of your branch.
Wingspan wide.

Jorge Mendez

Dive into the wind,
conquer the
heavens.

Today you learn
you've had
the ability to fly
for quite
some time now.

The Last Laugh

Have you ever laughed so hard
it made your sides hurt?
Have you ever found something so
absolutely hilarious
that your eyes tear up,
and your cheeks become sore?
Have you ever laughed so uncontrollably
that your stomach knots up,
your face aches,
you find it difficult to breathe,
and you think for a second
that you may just literally die laughing?

Have you ever been laughed at?
Not laughed with-- laughed at.
Like you're funny?
Have you ever been the butt of a joke?
People laughing so hard
it makes their sides hurt?
Have you ever been a punch line?
Punched in the spine so viciously
that your eyes tear up,
and your cheeks become sore?
Have you ever been humiliated so terribly
that your stomach knots up,
your face aches,

Jorge Mendez

you find it difficult to breathe, and
you think for a second that you wish
they'd all just literally die laughing?

Have you ever been a source of amusement?
Like a carnival.
Have you ever been someone's quick thrill,
someone's rush of adrenaline?
Boarded, exited, and forgotten before your passenger even made it
to the next ride?
Have you ever been a roller coaster?
Have you ever blazed down the track?
Have you ever derailed?
Have you ever been shut down for repairs?

Have you ever been a losing raffle ticket stub?
Have you ever felt random
like the numbers on a losing raffle ticket stub?
Only valuable with a prize attached.
Have you ever been torn along your edges?
Ripped right through your middle like a losing raffle ticket stub?
Have you ever been a loser?
Clumsy handed turning all you touch to dust?
Have you ever been a fumble?
Something someone let slip through their fingers?
A lost opportunity?
Have you ever been lost?

Have you ever held on?
Have you ever gripped so tightly to the monkey bar

that it kept you from reaching out to the next rung?
Have you ever just hung there?
Dangling, just as terrified of moving forward as you are of the fall?
Exhausted with worry over what they might think?
Afraid they'll all start laughing?
Plagued,
Dear God, what if they start laughing?
What will I do if they start laughing?

But who cares?
Who cares if they start laughing?

When was the last time you laughed?
Have you ever thought about what you sound like
when you're happy?
Have you ever thought of what it would be like to fall in love
with your own laughter?
Have you ever been so happy
that you laugh for no damn reason?
Have you ever been so full of joy
that it makes your sides hurt,
your eyes tear up,
and you smile so uncontrollably
your cheeks become sore?

Have you ever had the last laugh?
Have you ever put yourself first?
And have you ever noticed
how funny it all is,
when you really think about it?

Jorge Mendez

10 Reasons

Top Ten Reasons to Love Yourself:

1. You are you.
2. You are you.
3. You are you.
4. You are you.
5. You are you.
6. You are you.
7. You are you.
8. You are you.
9. You are you.
10. You are you.

About the Author

Jorge Mendez is a poet, musician, and spoken word artist based out of Hampton Roads, VA. He has been the standing host of the weekly "Monday Night Open Mic" at The Venue on 35th in Norfolk since 2012. He currently serves as Vice President of the Poetry Society of Virginia (Southeastern Region) and works in various areas of the arts community in Hampton Roads. His talents have led to opportunities teaching creative writing and performance including being Performance Coach for the 2023 Verb Benders Slam Team, a presenter at The Hampton Roads Writer's Conference, as well as a guest teacher at The United States Naval Academy in Annapolis.

Jorge started writing poetry as a child, later putting the skill he gained as a page writer into Hip-Hop format releasing 3 independent albums with long time producer and partner John "Smiles" Dennis on an independent recording label they founded called UKNODACREW Productions in 2002. He has since graduated to Spoken Word and has been performing his poetry at flagship events like Last Tuesdays, Arts Out Loud, Mic Fiend, Busboys & Poets, Push Comedy Theatre, and Verses & Vibes. In 2015, he created Poet Fest 757, an all-day poetry festival held annually during National Poetry Month.

In March of 2016 Jorge published a book of his works titled "Keys & Crowbars" released on San Francisco Bay Press, followed by Candy and Rigor Mortis Vol. 1 and 2 which he co-authored with JT Williams.

Jorge Mendez has become a well-respected staple of the Hampton Roads Performance Poetry community as well as a mentor for many new artists.

Jorge Mendez

colophon

Look for Jorge Mendez's 1st volume of poetry "Keys & Crowbars" from San Francisco Bay Press and his co-written Horror Anthologies Candy & Rigor Mortis 1 & 2 (and beyond) with J.T. Williams from Wider Perspectives.

These poets, novelists, tale-tellers, and memoirists have supported Wider Perspectives throughout and all deserve your curiosity and patronage, seek them out on the internet, order their books, request their books at booksellers near you or from Wider Perspectives. Many are visible on FaceBook, Instagram, the Virginia Poetry Online channel on YouTube:

Travis Hailes- Virgo, thePoet
Nick Marickovich
Grey Hues
Madeline Garcia
Chichi Iwuorie
Symay Rhodes
Tanya Cunningham-Jones
    (Scientific Eve)
Terra Leigh
Raymond M. Simmons
Samantha Borders-Shoemaker
Taz Weysweete'
Jade Leonard
Darean Polk
Bobby K.
    (The Poor Man's Poet)
J. Scott Wilson (Teech!)
Charles Wilson
Gloria Darlene Mann
Neil Spirtas
Jorge Mendez & JT Williams
Sarah Eileen Williams
Stephanie Diana (Noftz)
Shanya – Lady S.
Jason Brown (Drk Mtr)
Ken Sutton
Crickyt J. Expression

Se'Mon-Michelle Rosser
Lisa M. Kendrick
Cassandra IsFree
Nich (Nicholis Williams)
Samantha Geovjian Clarke
Natalie Morison-Uzzle
Gus Woodward II
Patsy Bickerstaff
Edith Blake
Jack Cassada
Dezz
M. Antoinette Adams
Catherine TL Hodges
Kent Knowlton
Linda Spence-Howard
Tony Broadway
Zach Crowe
Mark Willoughby
Martina Champion
... and others to come soon.

the Hampton Roads
    Artistic Collective
    (757 Perspectives) &
The Poet's Domain
are all WPP literary journals in cooperation with Scientific Eve or Live Wire Press

www.ingramcontent.com/pod-product-compliance
Lightning Source LLC
Chambersburg PA
CBHW071607170426
43196CB00033B/2120